Dd

Hh

Jj

Gg

Ff

Aa

Ii

Tt

A CHILDREN'S BOOK
OF
TONGUE TWISTERS, POEMS &
RIDDLES FROM A TO Z

Writen by David Marango
Illustrated by Jennifer Marango

AuthorHouse™
1663 Liberty Drive, Suite 200
Bloomington, IN 47403
www.authorhouse.com
Phone: 1-800-839-8640

AuthorHouse™ UK Ltd.
500 Avebury Boulevard
Central Milton Keynes, MK9 2BE
www.authorhouse.co.uk
Phone: 08001974150

First published by AuthorHouse 8/9/2006

ISBN: 1-4259-4026-9 (sc)

Library of Congress Control Number: 2006905068

Printed in the United States of America
Bloomington, Indiana

This book is printed on acid-free paper.

Bloomington, IN

author**HOUSE**

Milton Keynes, UK

Introduction

This book is skillfully and masterfully filled with brilliant colors and fine art. It not only teaches children their alphabet, but also teaches them good writing skills. This book is good for children and parents alike. It's filled with funny tongue twisters, cute poems, and guessing riddles. This book not only teaches children how to read, it also teaches parents the value of spending quality time with their children, being proud that they're getting a good education and having fun with it.

So, parents, sit by your children and watch their faces glow as they laugh, learn and spark their imaginations!

"The imagination of a child is like a rose. Once it is planted, it grows to be the most beautiful flower of them all."

Jennifer Marango

<u>Acknowledgments</u>

I would like to thank my 9th grade teacher, Mrs. Naftsinger,
for teaching me how to never give up and go for the goal!
I would also like to thank my 11th and 12th grade teacher, Mrs. Shields,
for believing in me when I wanted to give up.
And most importantly, I give all of my thanks to my Heavenly Father
for giving me the wisdom to make this book!

David Marango

I would like to thank my brother, David, for giving me the opportunity
to draw for this book. It has given me great pleasure and something to be
proud of!
I would also like to thank my church family from Eagles Wings Ministries for
having faith and believing with us that this book would be published.
I too would like to thank my God and Father for blessing me with the gift
of drawing and having much computer knowledge to make this book possible.
Also, thanks Mom and Dad for supporting us 100% of the way!

Jennifer Marango

Dedication

Dedicated to our one and only
precious niece,
Samarah Shiann Marango
Also dedicated to my one and only goddaughter,
Alexis Anne Charbonneau
and her new brother,
Christian Joseph Charbonneau

ⅴ

Aa

Apples, apricots, acorns and apes.
These are some of the words that begin with "a".
As you read each word, see how many words
you can spot that begin with "A" and "a".

Bb

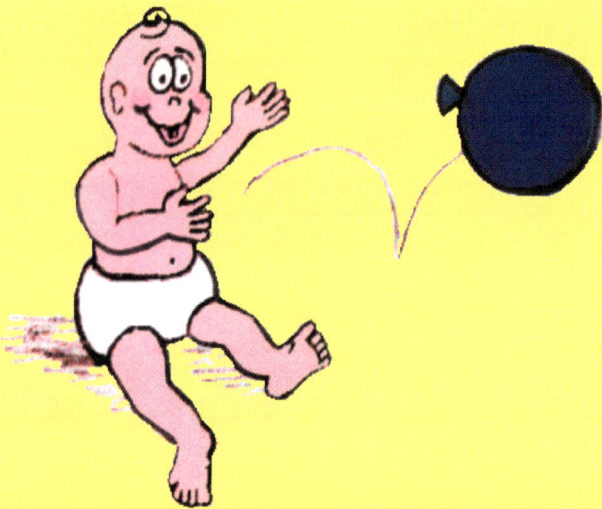

Baby boy Bob likes to bounce the beautiful, bouncy, blue balloon on the basement floor. When baby boy Bob bounced the beautiful, bouncy, blue balloon on the basement floor, the balloon blew onto a brown broom with lots of bristles and broke the beautiful, bouncy, blue balloon. The noise scared baby boy Bob so much, that he broke down and cried to hear the beautiful, bouncy blue balloon go boom!

BOOM

Cc

I am a vegetable. My body is orange.
Rabbits like to eat me all the time.
People like to put me in the beef stew.
I help you see good if you eat enough of me.
What am I ?

Dd

Ducks like to swim. Ducks like to hide.
Ducks like to fly up high and touch the morning sky.

Ee

Edgar, the elephant, eats elegant eggs.
Edgar eats the eggs with excitement.
Edgar's ears extend in the air when he
eats the elegant eggs excitedly.

Ff

I am an animal. My skin is green.
I like to jump on water lilies and eat flies.
Fairytales say I will become a prince if you kiss me.
What am I?

bounce
bounce

G g

Grapes are good. Grapes are great.
Eat those grapes on a plate.
Grapes have three colors: purple, green, and red.
I prefer to eat the green grapes than the other two instead.

Hh

Hats, hats, wonderful hats.
Hats for riding, hats for hiking.
Hats, hats, wonderful hats.
Choose whatever hats you like for styling.

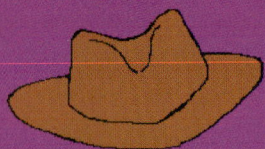

I i

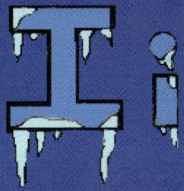

I am white. I am made of ice.
I keep people warm in the winter.
People make fires in me.
People go fishing under me.
What am I ?

We are a food. We come in many colors and flavors.
We end up in your Easter baskets on Easter day.
What are we ?

K k

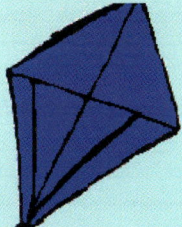

Kites, kites, I like to fly kites.
Kites with long tales, kites with long veils.
Kites, kites fly high in the sky.
Don't let go of my hand, or I'll have to say goodbye.

Lazy lambs like licking lollipops on Lemon-Lime Lollipop Lane. While licking their lollipops, they saw a large lion laying on the lime-green lawn. The large lion woke up to see the lazy lambs licking lollipops on Lemon-Lime Lollipop lane and laughed a lot.

M m

I am a drink that comes in three flavors.
I go in peoples coffee or tea. You like me with cookies.
You even put me on your cereal.
What am I ?

Nn

Needles under cushions. Needles on the floors.
Needles lying everywhere, except in needle drawers.

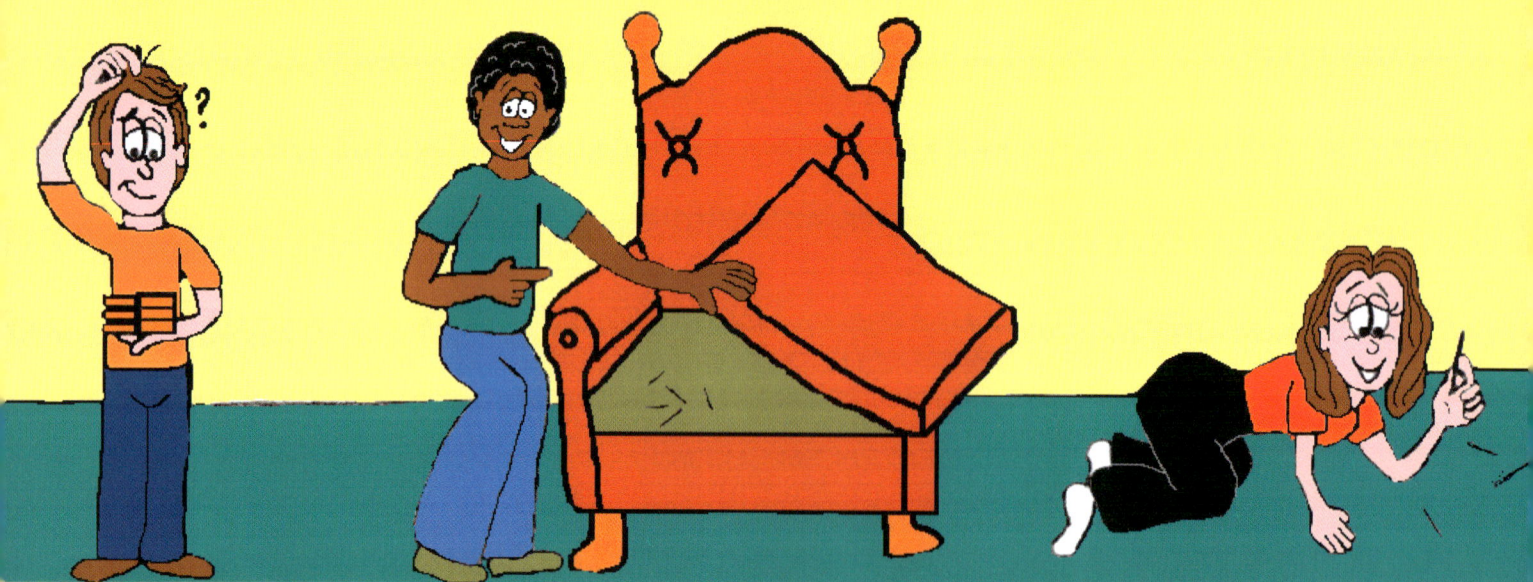

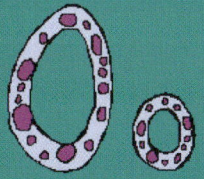

I am an animal. I live in the ocean.
I have many arms and legs.
When someone tries to hurt me, black ink
comes out.
What am I ?

P P

Pirates are scary. Pirates are mean.
When pirates feel sick, their faces turn green.

GRRR

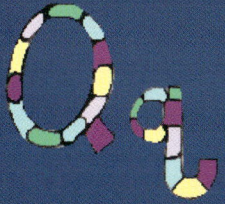

I am a thing. I like to keep you nice and warm.
I come in many colors.
People put stitches on me to make a beautiful design.
What am I ?

Rr

Ralf is a rabbit who likes to eat and play.
He runs, an jumps, and spins around,
chasing his tail all day.

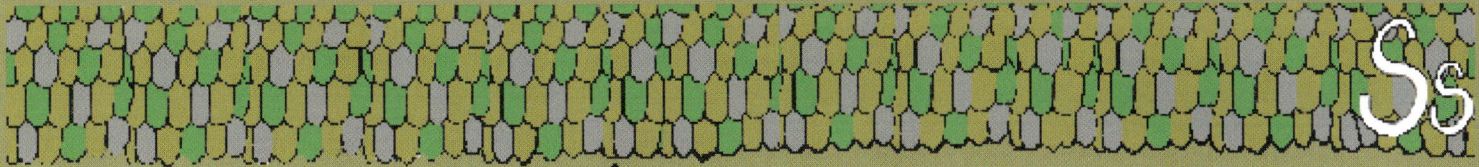

Scales

Long

I am an animal. I can be long, short, or fat.
My skin is scaley. I slide on my belly to get around.
What am I ?

SHORT

FAT

T +

Tarts, tarts, tasty tarts, ten or twenty a tray.
Tangy and sweet! Oh! What a treat!
Why don't you try one today?

U u

I am a thing. I keep you dry in the rain.
My head is like a big hat.
What am I ?

Valentines day is a sweet holiday.
It's a time to get cards, chocolates, and hearts.
How many cards did you get today?

Glass ←

Ww

I am a thing. I am made of glass. I live in your house.
You open me when you are hot and close me when you are cold.
What am I ?

OPEN

CLOSE

X x

HOSPITAL

I am a machine . I am found in a hospital.
When you are hurt, I take a picture of your skeleton.
What am I ?

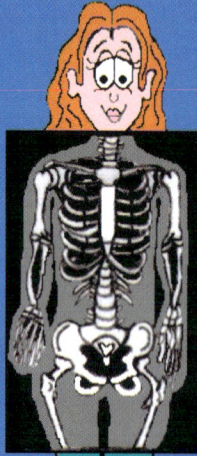

Yy

Yo-yos go up. Yo-yos go down.
I can do yo-yo tricks, and make it go all
around.

Zz

I am an animal. I can live in a zoo, or in the wild.
I look like a horse with black and white stripes.
What am I ?

neeigh!

Printed in the United States
82728LV00002B